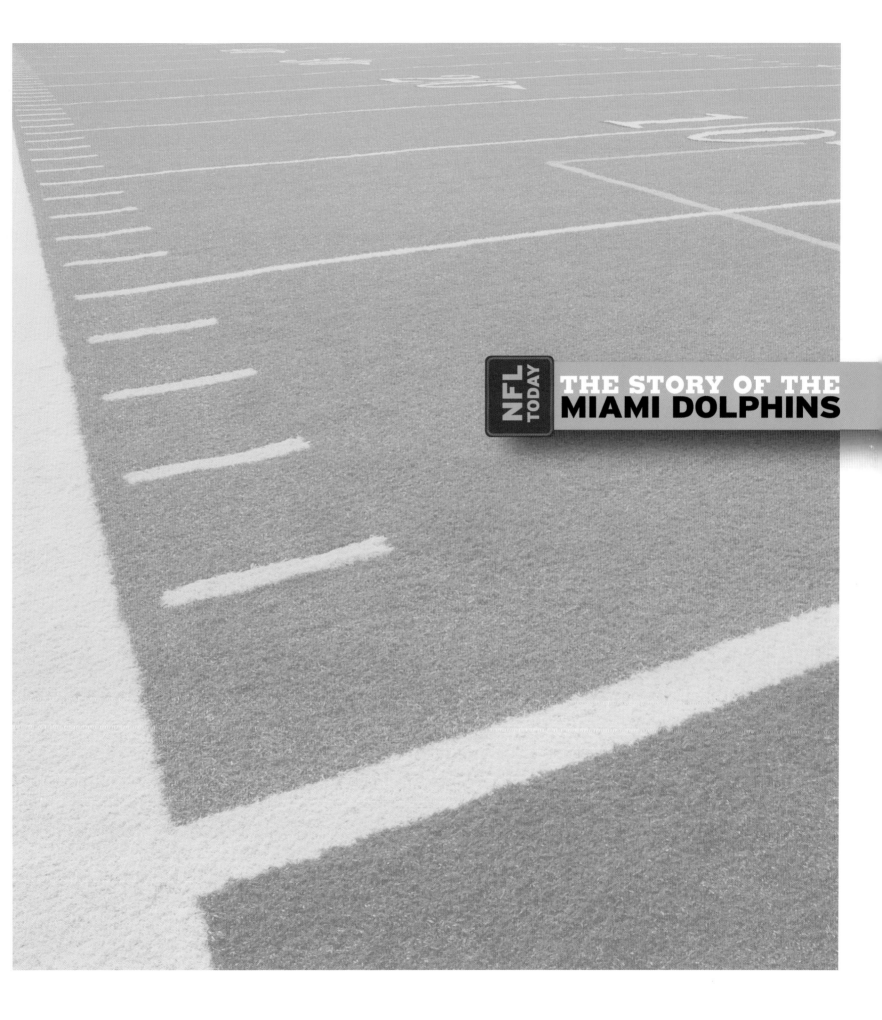

NFL
TODAY

THE STORY OF THE
MIAMI DOLPHINS

NFL TODAY

THE STORY OF THE

MIAMI DOLPHINS

SCOTT CAFFREY

CREATIVE EDUCATION

Cover: Quarterback Dan Marino (top), Dolphins offense, 2008 (bottom)
Page 2: Running back Patrick Cobbs (top) and offensive tackle Jake Long (bottom)
Pages 4–5: 1982 Miami Dolphins
Pages 6–7: Defensive end Jason Taylor

Published by Creative Education
P.O. Box 227, Mankato, Minnesota 56002
Creative Education is an imprint of
The Creative Company
www.thecreativecompany.us

Design and production by Blue Design
Design Associate: Sarah Yakawonis
Printed in the United States of America

Photographs by Corbis (Atlantide Phototravel, Vick McKenzie/NewSport, Norbert Wu/Science Faction), Getty Images (Doug Benc, Bruce Bennett Studios, Focus On Sport, George Gojkovich, Sam Greenwood, Rod Hanna/NFL, Walter Iooss Jr./Sports Illustrated, Allen Kee/NFL, Kidwiler Collection/Diamond Images, MJ Kim, George Long/NFL, John G. Mabanglo/AFP, Takashi Makita/NFL, Ronald Martinez, Al Messerschmidt/NFL, Ronald C. Modra/Sports Imagery, NFL, Darryl Norenberg/NFL, JC Ridley/NFL, Bob Rosato/Sports Illustrated, George Rose, Manny Rubio/NFL, Rhona Wise/AFP)

Library of Congress Cataloging-in-Publication Data

Caffrey, Scott.
The story of the Miami Dolphins / by Scott Caffrey.
p. cm. — (NFL today)
Includes index.
ISBN 978-1-58341-761-4
1. Miami Dolphins (Football team)—History—Juvenile literature. I. Title. II. Series.

GV956.M47C35 2008
796.332'6409759381—dc22   2008022688

First Edition
9 8 7 6 5 4 3 2 1

CONTENTS

X

X

ON THE SIDELINES

MEET THE DOLPHINS

GREEN GRASS
AND SUNSHINE

x- -

With year-round sunshine, beautiful beaches, and a tropical temperature, the city of Miami, Florida, is the closest thing to paradise on America's East Coast. In the 1920s, Miami experienced a population explosion as Americans flocked southward. In the 1960s, many Cubans immigrated there, creating a large Spanish-speaking population. Today, Miami is a popular destination city for vacationers, celebrities, and sports fans alike.

In 1965, Minnesota lawyer Joe Robbie brought professional football to Miami in the form of a new American Football League (AFL) franchise. When it came to choosing the team's name, Robbie held a newspaper write-in contest. Nearly 20,000 entrants offered up more than 1,000 different names, including the Sharks, Moons, and Suns. The most popular choice was "Dolphins," a sea mammal native to Florida's coast. "It makes sense," Robbie explained. "The dolphin is one of the fastest and smartest creatures of the sea."

In the Dolphins' first season in 1966, hopes for success ran high, especially after speedy running back Joe Auer returned the opening kickoff of the first game 95 yards for a touchdown. But that was one of few exciting Dolphins performances that year, as the team struggled to a 3–11 record. Miami's first coach, George Wilson, had little talent

X Wide beaches and an abundance of fine hotels and cruise lines have made Miami a vacation destination for many; since 1966, the Dolphins have made it a famous football town as well.

with which to work, but he found reasons for optimism in players such as offensive tackle Norm Evans, who established himself as one of the AFL's best linemen.

Things began to change for the better in 1967 when Miami drafted Bob Griese, a talented quarterback from Purdue University. Griese had great intelligence and superb instincts. Combining those attributes with a strong throwing arm and unparalleled poise under pressure, he quickly emerged as the team's leader. Griese helped Miami improve by only one win in 1967, but his promising play gave fans hope.

The Dolphins added balance to their offensive attack when they selected two running backs in the 1968 NFL Draft—a battering ram of a fullback named Larry "Zonk" Csonka and an equally powerful halfback named Jim Kiick. Csonka's bruising lead blocks combined with Kiick's quick feet to give Miami a formidable backfield. Thanks to this new duo, the team improved to 5–8–1 in 1968.

When Miami slipped back to 3–10–1 in 1969, it marked the end of Wilson's coaching tenure in Miami. Although he had trouble getting the Dolphins to win, Wilson's enduring legacy would be his ability to stockpile elite talent. During his time in Miami, he signed many players who would become Dolphins stars, including running back Eugene "Mercury" Morris, guard

BOB GRIESE

QUARTERBACK
DOLPHINS SEASONS: 1967-80
HEIGHT: 6-FOOT-1
WEIGHT: 190 POUNDS

Known as "the thinking man's quarterback," Bob Griese was renowned for his leadership skills and poise under pressure. He was also known for wearing glasses. It was an unconventional look, but it wasn't just Griese's eyewear that convinced people of his intelligence. Rather, it was his all-out effort and knack for calling the right play at the right time that set him apart from other quarterbacks of his era. "One of my strong suits as the quarterback of the Miami Dolphins was preparation," Griese later said. "I would pore over game films and dissect defenses. I knew every tendency of a defense going into a game." That kind of diligent preparation allowed the Dolphins to run the ball more and forced Griese to become more of a game manager with fewer passing opportunities. But Griese didn't care how the Dolphins picked apart defenses as long as the result was a victory. As Dolphins coach Don Shula said, "He got as much of a thrill calling the right running play for a touchdown as he did connecting on a bomb."

LOOK! LIVE DOLPHINS!

In the early days, the Miami Dolphins didn't win many games, and very few fans showed up in the late 1960s at the Orange Bowl to watch them. As a way to draw fans, the team kept a live dolphin named Flipper in a pool at one end of the stadium. Flipper was the Dolphins' first official mascot, but his sideshow antics weren't enough to put people in the seats. Miami kept losing, the fans stayed away, and eventually, Flipper lost his job because it became too expensive to keep him on the premises. These days, the Dolphins maintain their live-dolphin connection through an association with Key Largo's Island Dolphin Care Center, a facility owned by a nonprofit organization that provides dolphin-assisted therapy to children with special needs all over the world. The "Miami Dolphins Learning Hut" at the center was built from donations to the Miami Dolphins Foundation. The Hut contains a hands-on, open-air aquarium that houses different sea creatures native to Florida. Dolphins players have been known to visit the Center in the off-season to enjoy the unique opportunity of swimming with the dolphins.

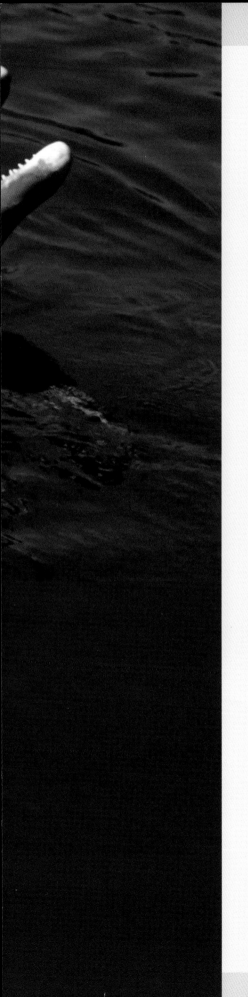

Larry Little, and defensive back Dick Anderson. In addition,
Wilson took a chance on undrafted defensive end Manny
Fernandez in 1968 and traded for linebacker Nick Buoniconti
in 1969. Both would later prove to be big-game playmakers.

The turning point for the Dolphins came in 1970, when
Robbie made two important moves. First, Miami boosted its
offense further by trading a first-round draft pick to the
Cleveland Browns for dangerous receiver Paul Warfield. But
it was the second move, luring coach Don Shula away from
the Baltimore Colts, that had the biggest impact. Shula
made it clear right from the start that he expected to build a
champion in Miami. "My goals are the same every year—to win

X A Pro-Bowler in
1971, 1972, and 1973,
undersized halfback
Eugene "Mercury"
Morris often served as
a backup to Jim Kiick
but also starred as a
kick returner.

the Super Bowl," he said. "And we'll do just that."

Shula wasted no time in transforming the struggling Dolphins into a powerhouse. In 1970, as the AFL merged with the National Football League (NFL), Miami put together its first winning record (10–4) and earned a playoff berth. Although the Dolphins lost a hard-fought battle with the Oakland Raiders, 21–14, it was clear that Miami was ready to win.

A former college track star, Paul Warfield was one of the fastest receivers pro football had ever seen, averaging an astonishing 20 yards per catch over the course of his career. **X**

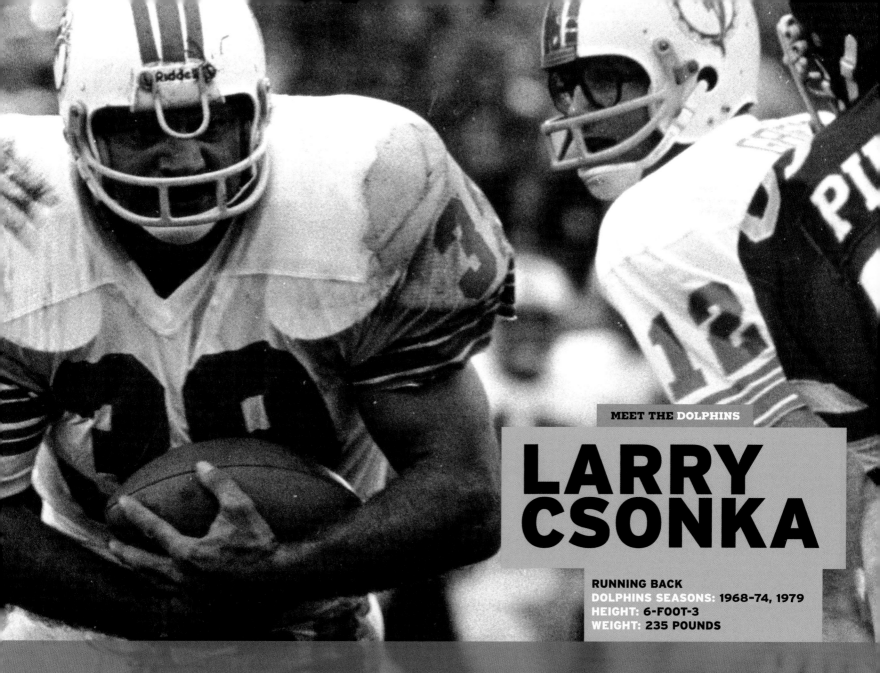

LARRY CSONKA

RUNNING BACK
DOLPHINS SEASONS: 1968–74, 1979
HEIGHT: 6-FOOT-3
WEIGHT: 235 POUNDS

Known for his throwback playing style, Larry Csonka was a reliable workhorse whom coach Don Shula could always count on to get the tough yards. He was the kind of player who "preferred to shake a little dirt out of my helmet," as he once said. And although he was fast enough to run around defenders, he preferred running *over* them. But Csonka wasn't just a great ballcarrier. He was also a bruising fullback whose blocks created wide holes for halfbacks Jim Kiick and Mercury Morris. "My role is to make the power running game work," Csonka said. "It's not a spectacular strategy, but I've lived and breathed it, and I know it works." Csonka made headlines when he made a money grab and signed with the Memphis Southmen of the new World Football League in 1975. But he returned to the NFL the following year and played three seasons for the New York Giants. For his last season as a pro, Csonka came home to Miami in 1979 and finished his legendary career where he started it.

[15]

THE PERFECT SEASON

X Although Miami's high-powered rushing attack in the 1970s meant that quarterback Bob Griese threw relatively few passes, he made them count, almost always finding the open man.

In 1971, after another 10-win season, Miami earned its first American Football Conference (AFC) East Division championship and met the Kansas City Chiefs in the playoffs. That game turned into a marathon contest that remains the longest game in NFL history at 82 minutes and 40 seconds. After the teams traded scores throughout regulation and then went scoreless in a first overtime, Dolphins kicker Garo Yepremian booted a 37-yard field goal through the uprights in the second overtime to give Miami a 27–24 win.

The "Fins" then proved they were no fluke by shutting out the Colts 21–0 in the AFC Championship Game. Although Miami lost Super Bowl VI to the Dallas Cowboys two weeks later, the team was primed for greatness. In the locker room after the loss, Shula implored his players, "We have to dedicate ourselves to getting back to the Super Bowl next season and winning it."

Shula never asked his players for perfection, but in 1972, that's exactly what he got. When Griese broke his leg and

DON SHULA

COACH
DOLPHINS SEASONS: 1970-95

Long before Don Shula became the winningest NFL coach of all time, he was the lone rookie on legendary coach Paul Brown's Cleveland Browns team. Beginning in 1951, Shula was a defensive back who helped Cleveland reach the NFL Championship Game in each of his first two seasons. In 1953, he was involved in the largest trade in modern NFL history, as one of 15 players swapped between the Browns and the Baltimore Colts. As a player, Shula earned the career totals of 21 interceptions with 247 return yards. But it was as a coach that Shula really made his mark on the game. His belief in a unified team allowed Shula to enjoy a long career with respect from players and fellow coaches around the league. "Football is a team game," Shula said. "It's not one or two people, it's everyone working together." Shula received countless awards, including the 1993 *Sports Illustrated* Sportsman of the Year Award and the 1994 Horatio Alger Award for his charitable contributions. His alma mater, John Carroll University in Cleveland, even named its football stadium after him.

dislocated his ankle in the season's fifth game, 38-year-old

backup quarterback Earl Morrall stepped in. Csonka and

Morris, meanwhile, took the offense on their shoulders as

each player rushed for more than 1,000 yards—a pro football

first for two teammates in the same season. While Morris

scored a league-high 12 rushing touchdowns, Morrall rounded

out the brilliant performance of the offensive trio as the

league's top-rated quarterback.

Miami's defense, meanwhile, was just as impressive.

Nicknamed "The No-Name Defense" because of its shortage

of star-caliber players, it allowed the fewest points of any NFL

X Linebacker Nick
Buoniconti (right)
was probably the
best-known player
on Miami's "No-Name
Defense" in 1972.

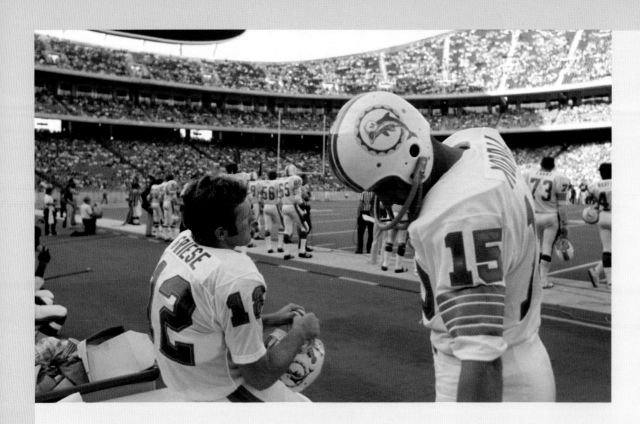

X Earl Morrall (right) stepped in for an injured Bob Griese (left) in 1972, then served as his backup for another four seasons.

team in 1972. "The nickname doesn't bother us," said safety Jake Scott. "I don't care if people remember my name as long as we don't have any losses." Scott's words proved prophetic as Miami finished the regular season a perfect 14–0.

In the playoffs, Miami led the Cleveland Browns for nearly three quarters. Cleveland jumped ahead 14–13 halfway through the fourth quarter, but the steely Morrall directed an 80-yard scoring drive to give Miami a 20–14, come-from-behind win. However, Morrall struggled the next week against the Pittsburgh Steelers in the AFC Championship Game. After he threw an interception, Shula pulled him and barked to the now-healthy Griese, "Get us out of here with a win." Griese started the heroics with a 52-yard strike to Warfield, and Kiick then scored two

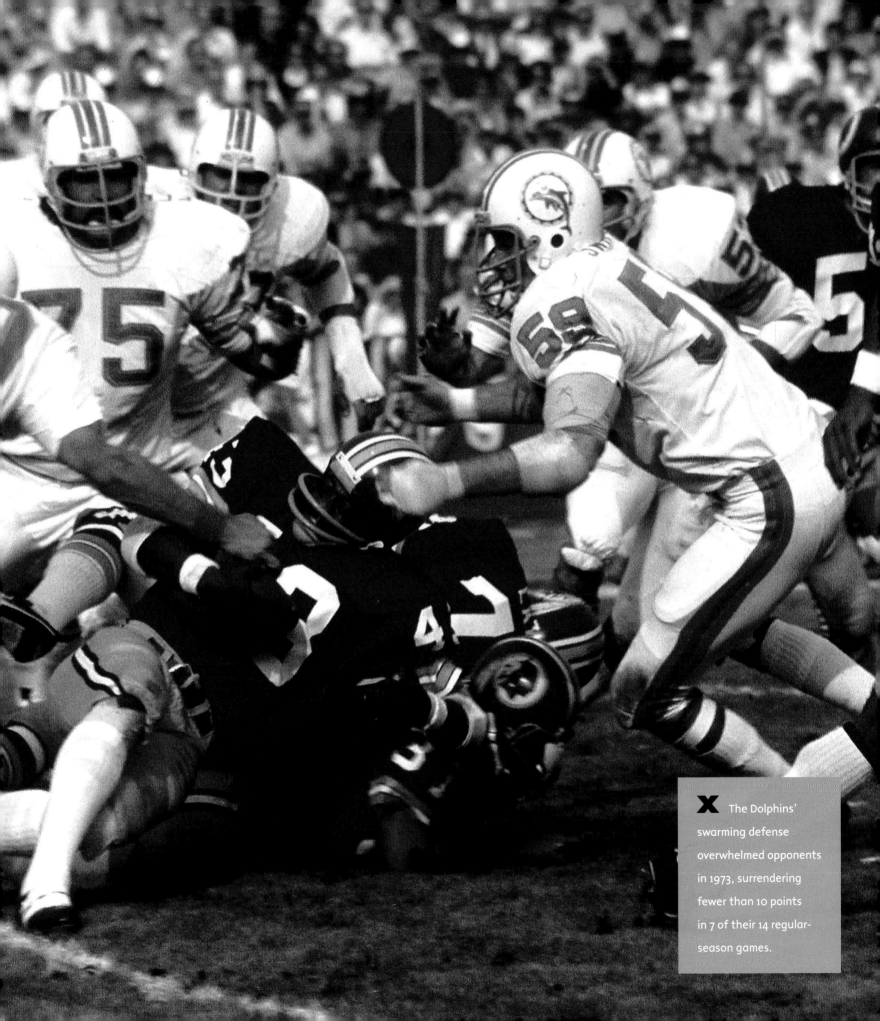

X The Dolphins' swarming defense overwhelmed opponents in 1973, surrendering fewer than 10 points in 7 of their 14 regular-season games.

GARO'S GAFFE

One of the most famous and bizarre plays in Dolphins lore came with two minutes to go in their perfect 1972 season. It was the fourth quarter of Super Bowl VII, and the Dolphins' "No-Name Defense" was protecting a 14–0 shutout over the Washington Redskins. Coach Don Shula looked to ice the game with a field goal from Garo Yepremian, his accurate and reliable kicker. But after a low snap from the long-snapper, Washington was able to block Yepremian's kick. Players from both teams scrambled for the loose ball, but Yepremian got there first and picked it up. In an attempt to keep the play alive, he tried to make a pass. The ball rolled off his fingers awkwardly, and he batted it forward ... right into the hands of Washington defensive back Mike Bass, who raced 49 yards for the Redskins' first touchdown. "I watched the whole thing on the sidelines, and I couldn't believe what I was seeing," Shula said. Fortunately for Yepremian, the No-Namers bailed him out by stopping Washington's final possession to preserve the perfect season.

touchdowns to give Miami a 21–17 victory and its second Super Bowl berth.

Amazingly, even though Miami was undefeated, most experts predicted that the Washington Redskins would win Super Bowl VII. But the Dolphins were determined to not have their perfect season ruined. The first half of the game was a defensive stalemate until Griese connected with receiver Howard Twilley to set up the game's first score. In the second quarter, Buoniconti snared an interception and returned it 32 yards. Soon after, Kiick plunged into the end zone to put Miami up 14–0 at halftime.

In the second half, the No-Namers rose up. On Washington's final offensive series, Manny Fernandez sacked quarterback Bill Kilmer for his 17th tackle of the game, then defensive ends Vern Den Herder and Bill Stanfill sacked Kilmer on the series' final play. The Dolphins won their first world championship with the first—and still only—perfect season in NFL history. "No question, our approach to this Super Bowl was much different from that of the previous year," linebacker Doug Swift said. "In Super Bowl VI, we didn't have our focus, but now we were intent on taking every play and every point seriously."

A NEW ERA

Elite teams always find a way to win. And the 1973 Dolphins seemed to find a different way to win each week. One game, cornerback Tim Foley was the hero, returning two blocked punts for touchdowns against the Baltimore Colts. Another game it was Warfield, who dominated the Detroit Lions by catching four touchdown passes.

Also that season, defensive coordinator Bill Arnsparger unveiled the "53 Defense," a scheme devised more out of necessity than innovation. Miami suffered a rash of injuries to its defensive line in the preseason. Forced to improvise, Arnsparger used linebacker Bob Matheson at defensive end but had him stand up like a linebacker. This gave Matheson the option of either rushing the passer or dropping back into coverage. The defense actually took its "53" name from Matheson's jersey number. The formation also put Fernandez over center, making him one of the league's first nose tackles.

The crafty Dolphins cruised to a 12–2 regular-season finish and crushed the Cincinnati Bengals 34–16 in the

Big and fearless running back Larry Csonka was like a freight train when he hit the line, making him the ideal ballcarrier in short-yardage or goal-line situations. **X**

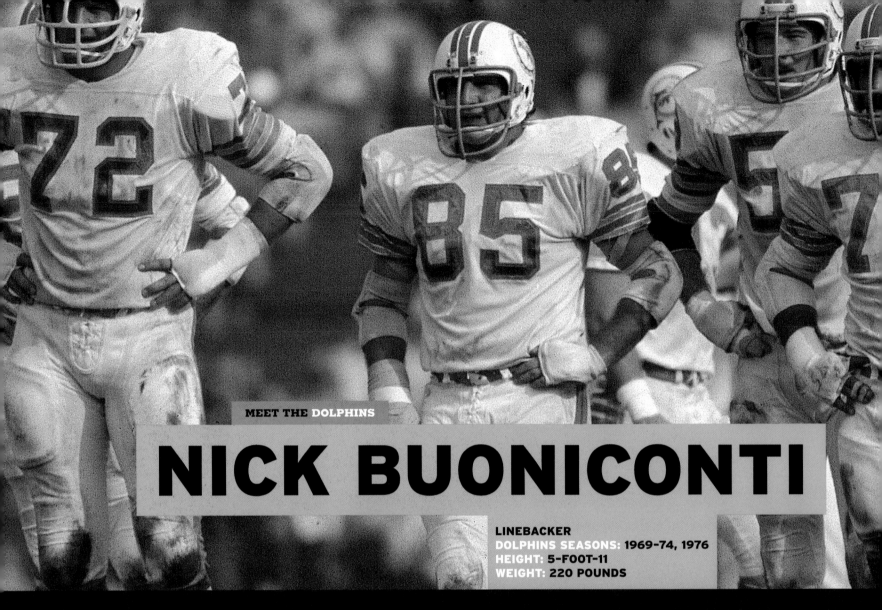

MEET THE **DOLPHINS**

NICK BUONICONTI

LINEBACKER
DOLPHINS SEASONS: 1969-74, 1976
HEIGHT: 5-FOOT-11
WEIGHT: 220 POUNDS

During his solid career as a two-way player (guard and linebacker) at the University of Notre Dame, Nick Buoniconti (pictured, number 85) was a natural leader who acted as the team's captain and was named an All-American his senior year. He carried those qualities into his split professional career—seven years with the Boston Patriots of the AFL, and seven with the Dolphins. No matter what team he played for, Buoniconti was a star. Before the 1970 NFL-AFL merger, he played in six AFL All-Star Games, including one with the Dolphins. Considered by many scouts to be too small to play middle linebacker, Buoniconti was widely known as a guy who "played bigger than his size." The driving force behind the vaunted "No-Name Defense," he made a distinctive mark in Miami during the franchise's glory years with well-timed, game-changing plays that helped his team twice garner football's ultimate prize. He also inspired teammates with his outstanding play and fiery leadership. "Every play is like life or death," he once said. Buoniconti was so respected that his teammates named him the Dolphins' Most Valuable Player (MVP) three times.

playoffs and the Raiders 27–10 in the AFC Championship Game, becoming the first team to advance to three straight Super Bowls. Csonka dominated the Raiders with 117 rushing yards and 3 touchdowns, and he kept on rolling in Super Bowl VIII. Running wild with 145 yards and 2 touchdowns, Zonk accounted for more than half of Miami's total offense, helping the Dolphins dismantle the Minnesota Vikings 24–7 for another world championship.

Miami won the AFC East in 1974 with an 11–3 record, but the Raiders proved that they were now an AFC heavyweight by narrowly beating the Dolphins 28–26 in the first round of the playoffs. That loss marked the end of a great era, as the franchise said goodbye to three of its brightest stars. Csonka, Kiick, and Warfield all left town to play in the newly formed World Football League.

Although Miami posted winning records in four out of the next five seasons, it lost both of its playoff appearances in 1978 and 1979. Still, Miami's impressive air attack—featuring new star receiver Nat Moore—kept the Dolphins exciting. In 1979, Csonka returned to Miami to frustrate opponents with his sledgehammer running style for one more year. Although that season ended with a playoff loss, it had been a remarkable decade for the Dolphins. Over the course of the

X A relentless nose tackle who often faced double-team blocking, Bob Baumhower was a steady defensive leader in Miami for nine seasons, making the Pro Bowl five times.

'70s, Miami had put together a combined 104–39–1 record and brought two Lombardi Trophies to southern Florida as Super Bowl champions.

By 1980, Csonka had retired, and Griese was starting to show his age. New leaders began stepping forward to keep the Dolphins flying high. One of these leaders was center Dwight Stephenson, an All-American from the University of Alabama. Hailed by coaching legend Paul "Bear" Bryant as "the best center I ever coached," Stephenson would be considered the NFL's premier center within a few seasons.

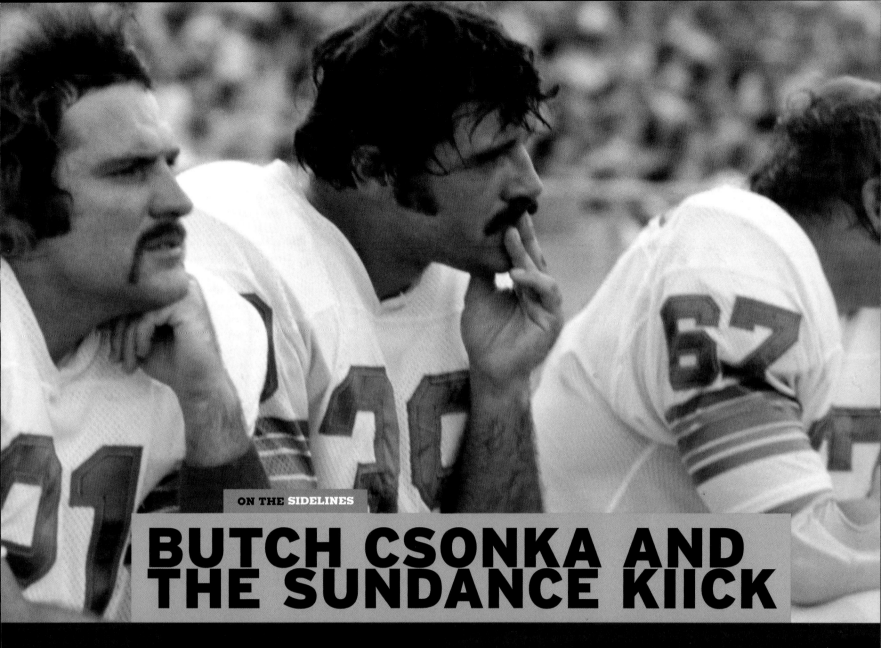

BUTCH CSONKA AND THE SUNDANCE KIICK

Dolphins running backs Larry Csonka (pictured, right) and Jim Kiick (pictured, left) wreaked havoc on the field. Off it, the best friends sometimes made even more noise with their pranks. In 1969, upon hearing of their exploits on and off the field, sportswriter Bill Braucher of the *Miami Herald* dubbed them "Butch Cassidy and the Sundance Kid," a reference to a movie about western outlaw buddies. In 1973, Csonka and Kiick even wrote a book together, *Always on the Run*, with sportswriter Dave Anderson. In it, they discussed their childhoods, college football careers, and experiences in the pros. They also detailed their sometimes rocky relationship with coach Don Shula. Many players were afraid of the stern Shula, but "Butch and Sundance" loved to push his buttons. Csonka claimed to have once thrown a baby alligator in Shula's shower and later, a black rubber hose that he pretended was a snake, just to get a rise out of their coach. "I still don't know who is who," Csonka said in 2003. "We managed to get in a lot of trouble all the time with everyone, so that's probably why we got that title."

In 1981, the fine play of Stephenson and nose tackle Bob Baumhower helped lead Miami back into the playoffs with an 11–4–1 record, but an overtime field goal by the San Diego Chargers ended Miami's season with a 41–38 loss. In a 1982 season shortened by a players' strike, Miami compiled a 7–2 record and convincingly thumped three playoff opponents (the Patriots, Chargers, and New York Jets), to earn its fourth Super Bowl appearance. Although the Redskins prevailed 27–17, it seemed that a major revival was in store for Miami.

DAN THE MAN

Catching passes
from Dan Marino, Mark
Clayton (pictured)
became one of the elite
receivers in football
in the 1980s, twice
leading the league in
touchdown catches
(1984 and 1988).

In NFL circles, 1983 was called the "Year of the Quarterback."

Five big-name signal-callers, including the Denver Broncos'

John Elway and the Buffalo Bills' Jim Kelly, were drafted before

Miami selected Dan Marino with the 27th pick. Although several

quarterbacks from that draft would become stars, none would

have the immediate impact that Marino had on the Dolphins.

"Dan the Man" was an NFL superstar as a rookie. In fact,

at season's end, he would be the starter in the Pro Bowl. "You

could tell right away that Danny had this unbelievable talent

to throw the ball," said Nat Moore. "He was so accurate …

[and] had so much zip on the ball. For me, playing with Danny

was more than anything like watching an artist at work. He

could pick apart defenses no matter what."

Marino picked defenses apart at an even greater

rate in 1984. By the ninth game, he had broken Bob Griese's

team record for passing yards in a season. With the help of

the sure-handed "Marks Brothers"—receivers Mark "Super"

Duper and Mark Clayton—Marino finished the year with new

NFL records in passing yards (5,084), completions (362), and

touchdown passes (48). This gaudy performance earned him

league MVP honors.

Assisted by the "Killer B's" defense (so called because

nine players' last names began with the letter "B"), the 1984

Dolphins rolled to a stellar 14–2 record. Defensive linemen Doug Betters and Charles Bowser kept pressure on opposing quarterbacks, and Miami's offense overwhelmed the Seattle Seahawks and Pittsburgh Steelers in playoff wins to put Miami in its fifth Super Bowl, this time against the San Francisco 49ers. Marino boldly predicted victory, but the 49ers defense shut down the Dolphins' running game and stunned Miami 38–16.

Miami reached the AFC Championship Game in 1985, but a 31–14 loss to the Patriots signaled the start of a late '80s slide. Despite the booming punts of Reggie Roby and the teeth-rattling tackles of linebacker John Offerdahl, the Dolphins missed the postseason every year the rest of the decade.

Then, in the early '90s, with vicious linebacker Bryan Cox bolstering the defense, Miami reappeared in the playoff picture. After shutting out the Chargers 31–0 in a 1992 playoff game, the Dolphins committed five turnovers in an AFC Championship Game loss to the Buffalo Bills. But the biggest heartbreaker came in 1994. After racing to a 21–6 lead over the Chargers in the playoffs, Miami was shut out after halftime and lost by one point, 22–21, after Dolphins kicker Pete Stoyanovich missed a 48-yard field goal with only seconds remaining.

LONGTIME WINNERS

From the 1970 merger of the NFL and AFL to 2008, the Miami Dolphins were the winningest team in professional football. They had the best regular-season (.623) and overall (.614) winning percentage of any team during that span. The team's regular-season record of 353–213–2 and overall mark of 375–235–2 stand above all others. The Dolphins were tied with the Dallas Cowboys for the most wins on Monday Night Football with 39 until 2007, when Dallas pulled ahead to 40. Even more impressively, by 2008, the Dolphins owned the second-best regular-season winning percentage of any team in the four major professional sports, behind only the Los Angeles Lakers basketball team. Although the Dolphins struggled as a young franchise, much of this overall ranking was a product of a great 1970s decade and years of consistent success. But as time marched on, the Dolphins slowly saw their lead as all-time winners shrink decade by decade. And while a 1–15 season in 2007 certainly didn't help their winning percentage, the 2008 Dolphins made up for it by rising above .500 once again.

[35]

DAN MARINO

QUARTERBACK
DOLPHINS SEASONS: 1983–99
HEIGHT: 6-FOOT-4
WEIGHT: 218 POUNDS

Dan Marino always shared a close bond with his father. Affectionately known around his Pittsburgh neighborhood as "Big Dan," the elder Marino taught his talented son the unique throwing motion that helped young Dan become one of the NFL's all-time great quarterbacks. Most kids are taught to extend their arm when throwing. But Dan's father taught him to hold the ball next to his ear, then snap his wrist forward to get the ball out quickly. As young Dan practiced his technique on telephone poles and street signs, it became clear that he had a special arm. His signature throwing motion helped him set passing records in high school and at the University of Pittsburgh. It also earned him immediate success as a pro. Marino was selected to nine Pro Bowls, more than any other Dolphins player. His record-breaking 1984 season led the Dolphins to Super Bowl XIX. And by the time he retired in 1999, Marino had set nearly every NFL quarterback record in the books. When asked if he could always throw so well, Marino admitted, "You know what? Yeah. I could flat-out throw it."

Despite that loss, 1994 was a special season for Coach Shula. After 32 years as an NFL head coach, he became the winningest coach in pro football history with a career regular-season record of 319–149–6. "His contributions to the NFL and the game of football extend far beyond his victory total," said NFL commissioner Paul Tagliabue. "Don Shula represents the highest standards of excellence by virtually any measure."

That same year, Florida businessman Wayne Huizenga bought the Dolphins from the Robbie family. He gave Shula a new contract, the title of vice president, and part ownership in the team. The newly motivated Dolphins went 9–7 in 1995 but were ousted by Buffalo in the opening round of the playoffs. Soon after that loss, Shula announced his retirement as coach.

To fill Shula's legendary shoes, Huizenga acted quickly to make Jimmy Johnson the third coach in team history. Johnson was a local legend, having led the University of Miami to a national championship in 1987. He had also rebuilt the Dallas Cowboys from a 1–15 mess in 1989 to a Super Bowl champion in 1992 and 1993. Johnson made it clear that losing was unacceptable. "I expect results," he said, "and as long as I get results, I'll be a very happy person."

SEASONS
OF CHANGE

The Dolphins slowly improved in the late 1990s under Coach
Johnson. He assembled a young, attacking defense that
featured middle linebacker Zach Thomas, defensive end Jason
Taylor, and cornerback Sam Madison. On offense, the veteran
Marino now slung the ball to speedy receiver O. J. McDuffie.

In 1998, Marino became the first NFL quarterback to
throw 400 career touchdowns. Yet despite his many passing
records, Marino still lacked what he wanted most—a Super
Bowl ring. He and all Miami fans were hopeful in 1999, when
the Dolphins started out 7–1, but the team stumbled in the
second half of the season. Although they beat the Seahawks
20–17 in the first round of the playoffs, their season came
to a jarring halt the next week with a 62–7 loss to the
Jacksonville Jaguars. Marino had an uncharacteristically poor
game, throwing two interceptions and being stripped of the
ball for a third turnover. In the process, Miami gave up the
most points in team history and suffered its worst loss ever.
Just days after the humiliating defeat, Johnson resigned
and was replaced by former Chicago Bears head coach
Dave Wannstedt. Marino retired, too, bringing his amazing
17-season career to an end.

With a sturdy defense still intact, Wannstedt rebuilt the
Dolphins' offense by adding veteran quarterback Jay Fiedler in

2000 and rookie wide receiver Chris Chambers in 2001. Then, in 2002, the Dolphins made the deal fans had been waiting for since Larry Csonka retired—they traded two first-round draft picks to the New Orleans Saints for star running back Ricky Williams. Williams arrived in Miami with the ultimate package of skills—strength, speed, vision, and aggression. "We've had big guys and fast guys, but not the whole combination," said running backs coach Joel Collier. "Ricky's not a talkative guy, but his actions make things kind of fun around here."

The Dolphins' single-season rushing record of 1,258 yards, set by Delvin Williams in 1978, had stood for 25 years before Williams shredded it with an NFL-best 1,853 yards in his debut season wearing aqua and orange. With tight end Randy McMichael catching passes over the middle of the field, and with the defense bolstered by veteran linebacker Junior Seau, Miami went 10–6 in 2003, just missing the playoffs.

Then, in a shocking development, Williams—who had run into trouble with the NFL over drug use—announced his retirement before the start of training camp in 2004. The unfortunate turn of events left Miami once again searching for an identity. At the end of that tumultuous season, Wannstedt was fired and replaced by Nick Saban, who had won the 2003 national championship at Louisiana

THE PERFECT REASON TO CELEBRATE

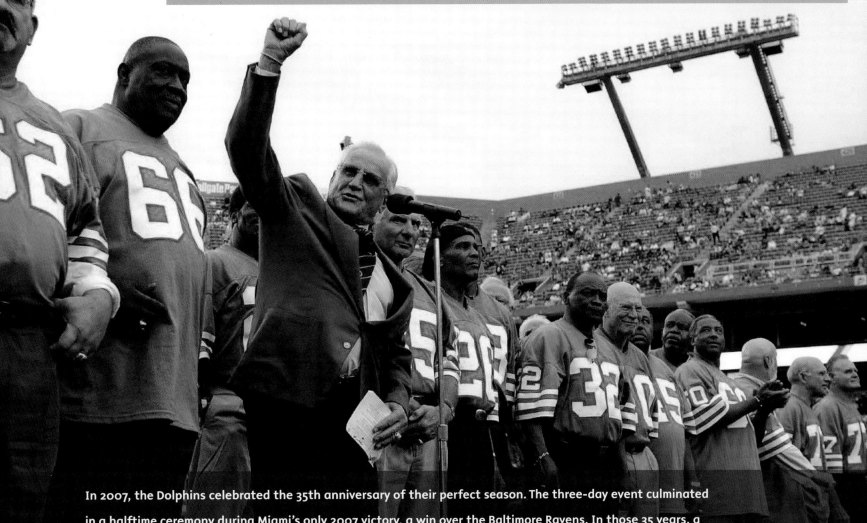

In 2007, the Dolphins celebrated the 35th anniversary of their perfect season. The three-day event culminated in a halftime ceremony during Miami's only 2007 victory, a win over the Baltimore Ravens. In those 35 years, a few teams have threatened to go unbeaten. But none came as close as the 2007 New England Patriots, who were a perfect 18–0 all the way up to their loss to the New York Giants in Super Bowl XLII. Rumor has it that, every year, when the NFL's last undefeated team loses, members of Miami's 1972 team gather to toast the loss. These rumors have given some outsiders the impression that they're grumpy old men who only wish ill on other teams. Coach Shula explained otherwise. "We're a happy-go-lucky bunch of guys …," he said. "I've always said if somebody runs the table, I'm going to call that coach and congratulate him. Until somebody else does it, we're proud of what we accomplished." Whether an annual toast actually occurs is uncertain, but many 1972 members do meet for a reunion every five years to catch up. After all, they have the perfect reason to celebrate.

X While coaches, quarterbacks, and running backs came and went in the first seasons of the new century, receiver Chris Chambers remained a steady performer.

X Ricky Williams's Dolphins career was a strange one; after great 2002 and 2003 seasons, he retired in 2004, only to return the next year.

State University. But Saban lasted only two contentious seasons before leaving for another college coaching job. His replacement, Cam Cameron, oversaw a miserable 1–15 season in Miami in 2007 before being fired.

Desperate for a turnaround, Huizenga brought in former NFL coach Bill Parcells as executive vice president of football operations and charged him with rebuilding the Dolphins. "We talk a lot throughout this league, and Bill Parcells is one of those names that if he comes in and he's on board, he's a guy that's going to get things going in the right direction,"

BIG JT

In 2007, when the NFL scheduled the Dolphins to play the New York Giants in its first regular-season game outside of North America at London's Wembley Stadium, it needed a creative angle to attract new fans across the pond. So the NFL built "Big JT," a moving, animatronic version of defensive end Jason Taylor, the Dolphins' reigning NFL Defensive Player of the Year, to strut the streets of London. Standing 26 feet tall and weighing more than a ton, Big JT was the biggest robot of its kind ever built. Each of his cleats was six feet long, and the football he held in his left hand was 25 times bigger than an official football. He was so lifelike and accurately proportioned that the uniform was created using exact NFL-regulated specifications. With a camera mounted inside his helmet, Big JT transmitted what he saw on a 40-foot television screen mounted behind him, which gave Londoners a unique perspective of their city. When he finished his walking tour, Big JT was the centerpiece of a tailgate party that also featured the Miami Dolphins cheerleaders.

ZACH THOMAS

LINEBACKER
DOLPHINS SEASONS: 1996–2007
HEIGHT: 5-FOOT-11
WEIGHT: 230 POUNDS

It is with good reason that Zach Thomas's favorite motto was "It's not the size of the dog in the fight, it's the size of the fight in the dog." Considered by many scouts to be undersized and too slow to play professionally, he answered critics by becoming the unquestioned leader of one of the NFL's most ferocious defenses in the late 1990s. "Coming into the league, I said, 'Just give me one year,'" Thomas recalled. Indeed, after starting every game but the opener as a rookie, he helped lead the Dolphins to five straight postseason appearances beginning in 1997. Thomas was the epitome of a fumble-inducing "run-stuffer." His secret was to get a quick jump on plays before his opponent knew what was coming. That instinct helped this on-field general set the Dolphins' team record for interceptions returned for touchdowns (4) and become one of only 3 NFL players ever to amass more than 100 tackles in each of his first 10 seasons. A seven-time Pro-Bowler with more than 1,500 career tackles, Thomas rightfully earned a place among the greatest defenders in Dolphins history.

defensive tackle Vonnie Holliday said. Parcells quickly hired Cowboys assistant coach Tony Sparano as Miami's new head coach. With Sparano leading such young stars as powerful running back Ronnie Brown, fleet-footed wide receiver and kick returner Ted Ginn Jr., and linebacker Channing Crowder, the 2008 Dolphins made big waves in the AFC East, capturing the division title in a turnaround that stunned the league.

In the span of four decades, the Miami Dolphins have written one of the most impressive stories in NFL history—five Super Bowl appearances, two world championships, and pro football's only perfect season. And with an all-time roster that includes such Hall of Fame names as Shula, Csonka, and Marino, fans have always found reasons to believe that their beloved Dolphins will soon swim to championship glory once again.

A 235-pound bruiser, running back Ronnie Brown helped the 2008 Dolphins go 11–5 and surge back into contention in the AFC.

INDEX